T0198562

WRITER

An AMERICAN Poet

KEVIN GREEN

AuthorHouse™
1663 Liberty Drive
Bloomington, IN 47403
www.authorhouse.com
Phone: 1 (800) 839-8640

Published by AuthorHouse 04/24/2020

ISBN: 978-1-7283-5156-8 (sc)
ISBN: 978-1-7283-5155-1 (e)

Library of Congress Control Number: 2020905318

authorHOUSE®

Intro

I wrote these poems to inspire myself and others to help guide the blind into the light of truth and imagination. Leaving behind truth of emotion, happiness, love, hate, fear and fantasy for all that may find my book a joy to read. I wrote this book to free myself for limitations and all of the stress and pain that life brings. Inside this book lies tales of life from the reflection of a true American Poet and still an ever present student of life, I hope you the readers enjoy my outlook on life, and experience another plane of conscienceness from a different angel of insight.

I bring to this collection of poetry that has been handed picked to entertain and inspire. I've been working day and night trying to create time to write and further mind my career as an American poet motivated by life and true emotion: It has been a great dream come true being able to become an inspiration to others. I am truly bless to have become a true American poet. I hope to inspire and leave you the reader with something to remember.

Summary

Thank you for reading, I am happy to bring to you a collection of poems that I have been working on for many years. It has been a great pleasure expressing myself through writing and rhyme trying my best to create a visual picture that inspires others. This collection of poetry that has been a great result and a true, dream come true. It has been a great fun coming up with ideas and creative motivation. I hope you the reader catch a feel and enjoy my outlook on life. I sincerely hope to entertain the scenes and leave the readers with something to remember forever.

I sincerely thank you

Kevin Green
    an
<u>American Poet</u>

<u>Trapped in a box</u> with no way out, I can feel the end closing in, trapped with no way out stuck in the box I'm in. I can feel the end getting closer sucking the life away stuck in this box of fright watching the time drift away. Slipping away with hardly any room to move or maneuver wondering how did I end up here, my brains in a stupier living in ignorance fear and fright stuck in a box with no light, not knowing if outside of this box is day or night, stuck frightened without light driving me to insanity I can feel the end closing in, with the cold breeze flowing over my skin. I can't win trapped in a box with no way out trying my best to move and clean myself out stuck in the dark in a box with no way out trapped in a box trying to claw myself out living a cruel life trapped in a box with no way out living in fear I can feel the end near, sucking the life from every breath I take trying to claw myself out with every move I make, digging in feeling my skin rip, while I try to rip through. I feel the end closing in as the wood splitters my bodily tissue trying to claw myself out feeling my blood soak through, dripping, on face stick, trapped in this box running out of space with the taste of my own seeping in, hating my life and the box I'm in. Running out of time, running out of space stuck in this box feeling the tears running down my face. I can't breathe. I can't see all I can do is hear the dreadful sound of crapping wood to bone and the sound of the beat of my heart and the cries of agony fright and fear echoes bouncing off the wood landing deeply in my ear, such fear such fright trapped in this box pleading for my own life stuck in a box with no way out trapped with no light I can't win feeling the blood from the top of the box dripping on my chin, feeling the wind from my own lung coating my chest I can feel the end getting nearer, I'm running out of breath, what did I do wrong to have my world end like this trapped in a small box with no room to move laying in my own clawing through the top of the box crying searching for home, trapped in this box with no light in a world all its own trying to crawl out this box that's is not my home. There must be a way out of this death trap clawing at the top of the trying to find my way out. Skin ripped to the bone, skinned alive trying my best to claw myself out trying my best to survive I can feel the end closing in offering the end of me, trapped in this box with no light I can't see. I can only feel the thumping of my own heart thump, thump, thump this and the tears falling down my face, and the blood soaked nine shavings falling all over my face, my hands numb finger bones clawing hot skin I can feel the end closing in hoping to make it out of the box of hell and nobody's around to hear my constant yells, nobody to help me in my search for life, nobody here to help me find the light, nobody here to help in my search for sight trapped in this box trying to claw to light suck fear not knowing if my action are for nothing I can feel the end creeping in I can feel the messenger of death closing in like the wind blowing over my skin I can't give up this can't be the end for me trapped in this box trying to hold me for eternity with unwelcome company stuck in this box with only my bones to accompany me. I can feel something on the other side, hands soaked with life I can feel the light hoping for a swallow grave not ready for the afterlife. I can feel the end closing in trapped in this box living in the world I'm in running out time taking deep breaths, clawing my way out trying to cheat death I found my way out skin to bone clawing to find my way out I finally found the light trapped in this box from dark to light, finally free at last living in after life.

Counting the tears falling down my cheek watching my life fall apart right in front of me, trying to put my life back together but the pieces don't fit. My life's falling apart and my knees feel weak, trying to put it together but I can't find the beat my heart skips a beat watching the tears fall down my cheek trying to put my life together but it feel like I'm missing a piece, its feels likes my heart and soul's on fire, somebody help me sooth my soul, watching my world fall apart knowing I'm not in control hoping I can put my life on hold hoping for somebody to hold me console me, help me in my time of need and never let go of me some to love me, to need me, someone to love and never leave me, someone to know me, believe me, love me forever and wont deceive me, watching the tears fall down my cheek hoping for someone to catch me when my body feels weak, when I'm weak in the knees hoping for someone to console me and fulfill my needs. Feeling so lonely I don't know what to do so I wrap up my tears and send them to you feeling so helpless I don't know what to do, feeling so sick for loving you, watching my tears fall on my pillow wishes they were you, staring at the wall seeing visions of you, so sick falling over you. I don't know what to do, sick in love, falling over you I don't know what to do.

I can feel the end closing with no light in sight hoping life in the afterlife stuck in the dark waiting for glimmer of light. There's no room out here for me, no space to breath no room to grow, no way out no truth to the life I live only lies and deception falsehood and fiction, no truth in the life I live except for the life I live trapped by lies that cross the lines of life, hoping for life in the afterlife with no end in sight hoping for the end to close in and take away the lies that surrounds me a life of lies that creep up to drown me while I can feel the end closing in with no end in sight hoping for end of torment and strains of life hoping for a life with reason a life with more meaning then this hoping for much more life than this. Surrounded by lies with no end hoping for something better waiting at my end I can feel the end closing in waiting for something better than the life I'm in.

Is it all an illusion, blinded by lives delusion of life and love, how could something so false feel so real. What a fool I must be, hoping the truth of life and love would set me free, what a fool I must be, consuming lies and deceit w??? Why this world sickens me, plagued by??? And mystery, with the eyes of agelessness. Nothing an ignorance is such bliss. Mocked by the figure that is in secret tell me, how priceless is the truth, and how does on put a price on love, materialistic untruths. Hold no value meaningless objects that lure me astray, delusions of life and love, cursed I am, cursed with this beating heart of mine, blinded by beauties life and I'm what a fool I must be, thinking love, could ever love me, is it love that sickens me, let the truth be told, feeling as old as the oak tree, still blinded by love, waiting for life to set me free, I can't believe life would make a fool of me. But then I <u>remember love is a part of life, and life is just a mystery</u>, or is it all an illusion. I find myself feeling so empty, trying to hold on to this emptiness, this nothingness that surrounds me, alone and hollow, holding on to the past, ignorance is bliss, but how long does innocents last, blinded by life, and love, watching lives delusions past, yes dear, I'll be here when the hours pass, is love just an illusion I dare to ask.

11-5-14

I am nothing, holding on to nothingness, that why I sometimes <u>Slip and Fall</u>

KG

When it all ends

I wonder what will we do when it all ends, running through life with the sky falling, look out below catch me in the wind no time to cry wolf, nowhere to run, nowhere to hide, we all dying on the inside with no time to hide, grab the nine and AK with no place to ride, what does it matter if we're all dying on the inside, emotions run deep we swallow our pride to hide the feelings that lie inside, hoping it doesn't all end, when it all ends trying to stay afloat when the sky starts falling, what do you do when the worlds collide, everyone fighting for life, step on, or be stepped on I wonder if any of it will even matter after we're all gone. Life goes on and moves on to the next chapter, we might lay in peace the next morning after, trying to keep it all together during this natural disaster. Knowing what happens now determines what happens after watching the tears fall watching the world turn against us all, watching everyone run for safety as the sky falls, dame who knew the world would turn against us all, running over you all, at the end of the world its save me fuck y'all, they trying to step on me to stand tall, running in circles holding on to life trying to stay strong, even at the end of life, life goes on, hoping life doesn't give up on me when it's time for the world to move on dame life goes on. Watching planes fall and crash and burn to ashes, ash to ash and dust to dust killing the next man for the life we lust, listening to the chaos that the world brings, listening to the flames sing. I wonder what will we do when it all ends, trying to stay afloat with the sky falling, life is life, until life is death its' hard to breath when your running out of breath. I'm not sure if it was a metro or something from once before, all we can do is hold on tight and endure life will never be like once before, if they change the value of money we'd all be poor, trying to live life like once before, trying to stay out of the rain when it starts to pour, run what for I can't breath and these ashes fill my lungs, waters turn acidic and blood runs cold, traumatized by life as the world unfolds life's cold and its getting colder, running from mother nature I think God told her, their looking for payback, they gave life just to take life back, a little taste of your own medicine, take that we're not the only ones that can't grow back, blood and tears mix in with this world of sin. I hope we're prepared to win, when it's time to end, the world stops the spin. Something from once before to bring this life to an end, as small as we are we can't win, the price of life for living in sin. I wonder what will we do when our world comes to an end, I wonder if we can ever start over again. Life is life until life moves on again, I wonder how it will all end, watching the worlds collide as the sky starts fallin, feed up, God and Mother Nature put us all in. life is life without life, who cares who's fallin payback I'm all in. The sky is fallin the sky is fallin that's death calling I'm all in where will you be when the world comes to an end. I hope when it's all over I can breathe again.

Poem: Mr. Dealer

Poker face

Playing the cards never knowing which cards will be played next hoping for the card that will give me the upper hand, a wining chance to make them all empty up, not being able to see the next card I pick up, hoping the aces are on my side hoping for a royal flush watching the cards slide. No jokers in the deck we play with aces high watching the hands of the dealer every time my cards slide bye. Playing the hand I'm dealt throwing in my chips, hoping for the chance to stack sky high every time the cards flip. Slide me another Mr. Dealer and count me in playing throat cut and I play to win. No grins, no frowns. Keeping my poker face on at all times, no time for second guessing when its chips on the line. So pass me another Mr. Dealer and let the chips fly playing the game to win every time the cards fly bye, poker face on no emotion stacking sky high sticking to the rules and regulations every time the cards slide bye. Making them antie up playing the cards right knocking down the competitions, no Mr. Dealer I'm not done yet stacking up my chips every time I bet waiting for any signs watching for the coming of dripping sweat. Keeping my game face on every time I play waiting for Mr. Dealer to reshuffle the deck, so slide me another Mr. Dealer the best hand I await starving for the game waiting for my next hand and I can hardly wait loving every time the cards flip, so slide me another one and Mr. Dealer don't slip, hoping for the Royal flush every time eyes on the cards and stacking chips on my mind, no second guessing I have to play my cards right holding the best hand with no competition in sight antie up I just might keeping my game face on playing the right with my poker face on, so slide me another one Mr. Dealer and give me a hand that I can understand playing the game right holding my cards in my hand.

Poem: 04-27-12

Somewhere between the lines of distant space, far from sight, right under your nose, not yet visible to you, where life seen from a different point of view, where there's is no instincts, and where everything old is new. There is no hatred here, only just, and righteous, a place where life can renew again, not apart from life to sea, there are some that wish they could take something they consider life from me those who blame their triumphs, and down falls on me, hidden in plain sight, between the lines of life, imaginary to those who dare not believe in sight. The unknown will never know what I am or, believe in what I can become, those that fear what you consider death, without changing what life is, those so young at heart, interested in those who change life to art, becoming a creator of sorts, molding life with every stroke of the pen, changing life with every brush of canvas, those who notice the change of the color of skin, mocking life, and time to maintain comfort for self, hidden in life the cure for illness in health, those to careless to care for self, only believing what one's eyes can see, there is a greater world behind the eye of the free from what you consider life and afterlife, creation where ideas are born and reborn to life, molding from the hands of the creator of life, there are closed channels for those with narrow minds, life left unseen by the eyes of mankind. Something to amazing for thought, much to comprehend. My life has no start, and life has no end, thought sent through space and time, to children so kind of heart. New life that begins to spark, where there's lines in life, man tends to arc, life should have no end, now begin to start. The truth hidden between the lines of life, careful some villains have need action, life to some is more than satisfaction learn what life is, and what life must become, on your journey there will be an end to so, between the lines of life, might contain a clue, you are partial to me, and I am all of you, until the time that life learn farewell a due, until learn life anew.

KG

Alternative (poem): 09-27-12

It's in my head, the meaning of life, madness engulfed by light, the sickening of lights and stage fright, the end of life, the end of light, that mangles the sight. It's in my head, behind the third eye of lead, capable of capturing the thoughts in my head watching blood of blue, bleed of red, oxygen toxifying the thoughts in my head why must I feel the pain of life wrapped in torment and torture like the brain of Christ. Fleeing life to return to light. It's in my head the madness within, deeper then flesh and the pain within. It's in my head I feel the pain over, and over again, release me now from this mental plain I'm in, one deeper than life and pain. It's in my head over and over again. Is it the reaper closing in, or is it the pain and torture that crept in. It's in my head over and over again. It's in my head life and light blinded by light even in after light. I need the pain to see what it is laying awake hidden deep inside of me. It's in my head watching blood turn to bloodshed ejecting the pain in my head, hidden deep within the third eye of life, pain is the rimmade to the light, and the afterlife. It's in my head, pain and bloodshed, tainting the soul that line the messages in the head. It's in my head, the end of life, the end of light, that mangles the sight. (It's in my head).

Poem

As frightful as life may become, one must never fear, for within the darkness the light is here, never needing to fear the unknown, there is nothing but truth in life. When one feels helpless in life, find truth in light, there is no fear so why fear the night. This is life with the absence of fright, bathed in the moon light, engulfed by light. There is nothing but truth in this unknown world of sight.

KG

Poem: 04-29-12

Death in the mist of sadness, buried by sorrow, only to live again, tortured by the chill, and the madness of the wind, non-existing by twilight with no ending insight. Trapped by the pattern of life, where does the pain end, sicken by the houles that blow in the wind, death sounds so sweet, the ending of pain, the beginning of peace, I shall no more be haunted by the beast. Hearing the winds call on me, peace shall come soon, with no end to me. Still in person, as the rains enter me, the chills and pains of life, that the winds sent to me, no sounds, no light, no clear of day to take away the sadness of day, ever so still, hoping for the madness to blow away. Take me away, the winds I say, away with all this madness and this sickening of life, is it only in death do I receive paradise, impatient for the afterlife or life, there must be a cure to what iles me, here in the mist of death, and sadness covered from head to toe in what man calls madness, if only I could fly away leaving to stay death disarray, confused by life and lives dismay, should one be reborn again, just to live life unwhole again, returning like the rains, replaying this life of pain, in love with sorrow, so comforting and home, here to live, and die alone feeling the near, and nearer then life, holding on to life preparing for the afterlife, no more pain shall come, here today, gone tomorrow as the rains come. Here and gone, I am me in mourn, not to blame its life to scorn, with only sadness, and madness to offer, the price for living, cursed until death takes me away. Free from now on, as the chill carries away. There must be much more to live for feeling the beat of the drum from beneath the earth core, sadness and dismay, temping as ever, here today gone tomorrow like the flight of a feather, life forever changing like the winds and weather changing like the seasons come and gone, remembering life as loving love song, here today gone tomorrow as life moves on, nonexisting by twilight, sickened by sight, sinking forever deeper in the mist of light.

Alternative poem: 04-30-12
Yesterday

I can't understand why my love wasn't good enough for you, embedded in the dark awaiting what waits for you, tell me why isn't love good enough for you, drunkened sadness lurks within my beating heart, not knowing when to end and when to start, is this empty love I feel burning in my heart, loves not good enough, feed up with your lies, sorry I've had enough, my love's not good enough, can you explain what went wrong, was it the sadness that trapped you so far away from this love song, <u>here today gone tomorrow that's all I have to say, no more madness, sorry loves gone away, she brought her heart back here yesterday, no more pain, sorry its gone away, your love hurts me deeply that's all I have to say</u>, remembering when my love wasn't good enough for you, broken hearted, crying over you, not knowing what to do, I was so in love with you, now it's all over and this is the end for you, sorry, my heart wasn't good enough for you, for the empty bottles, and lust that broke in two. Sorry that my love isn't good enough for you, this is the sadness, wrapped up in the madness, I was here patiently waiting for you, sorry love's over and this is the end of you, sorry my friend, sorry my loves wasn't good enough for you. Here today gone tomorrow that's all I have to say for you, no more lies, sorry my lives gone astray, that's all I have to say. She brought her heart back here yesterday, no more pain here in my heart. Sorry I've gone away, your love hurts deeply there's nothing left to say, here today gone tomorrow, so what happen to my yesterday

KG

Poem

What happen to tomorrow, there goes my yesterday, <u>drunken in</u> the madness, there's no love here to stay, smothered by sadness, there goes my yesterday hello to tomorrow, and good-bye to yesterday, my love gone astray, now good-bye to yesterday.

Poem: 04-31-12

Faith the destroyer of most, bringing the end of life for the sake of religion, when the truth is so far from heart. Scapegoats for life but who's really to blame, blaming life and limb, blaming the night, and dim blaming the words of him, blaming life for the life you took from him. How righteous thou must be, to be cleaned of conscience like he. Even in the end of me, you will never have the right of me, when the days come short to release the light in me. How can one believe in the existence of life and limb, and say you own the right of him. He who sacrificed his life and limb, cold faces of so called faith in this life of grim, to do it all again they would still take the life of him, because of the sacrifice of his life and him, would one so bold of faith, sacrifice your life for him, or watch death and dismay as they stone and turn life to dim. I can never say I am as right as him, but life doesn't mean as light as him, who is he who calls for peace of life, is it those who wish for his piece of life those who speak of truth and faith, those who choose to pick of fate to give and take. I am not the one to judge fate or the faithful, just living life so sweet and tasteful, giving thanks to those who remain truly grateful, blessed like those who remain truly faithful. What ever happen to love thy brother, tales of tailes from mans, son from mother to brother, will to will and let thy love thy mother, withhold from the fight between thy brother. Life I was told was the righteous and living, as life feeds off life, leaving the faithful praying and hoping for afterlife, condemning life from death because of fear and fright, putting the fear of God in thy heart because even life dies in the light. Room for the righteous and religion, forever grateful for what is life and living, what do I see, faith a destroyer of life, so called righteous life praying for the afterlife, I'm not the one to judge your right. I'm just a watcher observing the light.

KG

Poem: 04-31-12

Dying day after day sitting with this hole in my heart, living without you watching my world fall apart, putting together the pieces of a broken heart, this is the end, and I just don't know where to start, she gone again how can I go on living without my only friend, picking up wild roses blessed by your touch, how could I'll let go the one I've love so much, remembering the sweet rains and the tender warmth of her touch. Dying day after day, remembering the day I let my heart slip away. The woman that touched my heart, how do I mend this shattered, and broken heart, trying to catch memories of the past. Where do I start, watching the sand in the hour glass my love to pass, this time this love won't last, there's too much pain that remains, inside this broken heart of mine, they say all mortal wounds heal in time, no longer blinded by this love of mine, watching my world fall apart. I just don't know where to start, dying day after day sitting with this hole in my heart, how could I lose my only friend, remembering her dancing in the wind. She's gone again, and then the rain comes, tears from a broken heart, putting together the pieces of this broken heart.

KG

I once met a man who loved to share, he believed that women are meant for only an instant like a breath of fresh air, lasting only a moment in time, thinking if only this women was mine, man plus woman like before the beginning of time, only with a loving friend could I ever share this life of mine, but only for a moment in time, only if this women was mine.

KG

Poem 05-01-12

Life like food to the soul, forever existing, tight holds on life like water and air, in and out of life like a faithful prayer, layer of thought within and upon me, thirsting for knowledgement fit for the soul, now holding in my hands the key to life, longing for a life fit for life, immortalize by the knowledge that lie within, beauty deeper then thy own skin, soaking in the beauty of life, amazing in all ways, like the moon light that shines at the end of days. Always to return again, like life to whom to pale skin, braised by the light, mortality the food of life, existing but for only a minute of time, I stand the same as mankind, bleeding beautifully like a wonderfully aged wine, wise men say life become sweeter with time, is there ever enough time for life, asking the sun and the winds that become part of me, is there enough time after this life of me blessed thou are with every meal and glass of wine, blessed thou are for becoming part of time, life, food for the soul, engulfed by light as fate unfolds, beauty like the redest rose, hiding in secret stories yet to unfold. Stories yet untold, fate is foreseen listening to the stories wise men told, grateful are the old and wise, blessed by day to witness the sunrise witty in life, taking in the winds wondering about the beauties in life one does not always wait the afterlife to witness paradise all one has to do is take hold the beauty of life, food for the soul, the watcher watching the beauty of life unfold.

KG

Poem: 05-2-12

Stories of life brought here to sight, stories of dark seen by light, stories of men some great some sin in spite, men smothered by day seen by light, here lie tails of life, should on remain in the dark or become seen by light. I've once seen a man a begger to sight, an eye sore to some, but there's always a meaning to life, looked and frowned upon as a frown to life, what lies in the dark is always seen in light, no ordinary man, just frowned upon by life, no ordinary man, a man who's words brought meaning to life, trampled by public stubborn in life, no one to listen to a man who has seen the life, a man with words and the meaning to life, a man who has been through it all, from dark and brought fourth meaning to light, but who wants to listen to man less seen by life. I heard the man say that soon the end would come, I've seen it all, and this will be the end to some, then I heard the man say I have seen the light, even the dark is seen by light, protect your wives and your children, by the scene of night, for wickedness and destruction is foreseen by light, but the onlookers wouldn't believe in life no belief for a begger with esteem for life, laughing at a man who has seen the light, for I say I've seen the end, and its the end to come. Old man you've must have lost your soul in a bottle of rum, as the clouds started to roll in, watching the down pour close in, watching life consume life as the waters begin to shower, nah sayers gathering the children as the village people scatter, I've never seen a rain with such power, sweeping life away with in blink of an eye, watching life running from the sky, washed away by the waters and the winds, stories of life with life seen again no ordinary man of sight, this man who has seen the light, smothered by day seen by light, no ordinary man in this tail of life, what lies in the dark is seen by light, these stories of men, some great some of sin and spite, what lie in the dark can be seen by light. Only wise men heed the warnings of life.

2 more stories!!!

God, more greater then man, and the words of mankind, the creator of the sun. Here before so called life and death something much more then man, what thy eye can see, older then the moon, the sands of time, the wind and sea, impossible to contain the uncontainable image of the one, the creator of creation the one who holds the sun, through me you might here a story of life, find the good book and learn of the teachings of Christ, learning how life puts an ending to life, learning how the past, present can show you the future of life. To me personally is more than just the meaning to life, much more then wisdom and the known gift of sight, much more then darkness, and the gift to life. The Loving One who gave the gift to life, caring for forgotten soul swepted away afterlife. The One who must know all, the One who taught the stars, and the rains to fall, watching the world cry for me it seems, but something life feels just like a dream. The owner of fate it seems, the bringer of wishes and wonder dreams. I wonder if man can truly understand the meaning of life the true mean of earth, wind, water, fire, and ice, understanding that to He there is no death to life, the walker of different dimensions, the teacher to fire, and ice, the one to bring fourth energy to <u>Death</u> and <u>Life</u>, <u>to me peace and immortality is the meaning to life</u>, testing souls who dream to become the creator of life, understanding death is never to only peace to life, watching time melt away knowing my life is just a piece of life. Why must life continue to feed from life, praying for more meaning to life, slapped in the face by the many answers to life, why must one continue to need more than the meaning to life, greed followed by envy, jealousy, and sin answers blowing softly in the wind, wise men say seek and thy shall find, the answers to life and forgiveness of time. If one giving the ability to be free, then in time One will truly see Me God, much more then man, and the words of mankind. The creator of sun, the earth, time, and mankind, mastering mind and this creation of mine.

Poem: 05-6-12

Watching the reflection in the mist of the mourning dew, waiting to be born again, soaking the earth in mourn again, wet and yet still thirsting for life, a mirror image of life and paradise, another tear of God, life feeding on sadness, dew reflecting a perfect picture of life, and the colors of rain, here today gone tomorrow to be once more born again, finding meaning to this so called meaningless life here once again comes the beginning, the end to life, all under the heavenly sky, breathing in the moisture of the wind, under the falling sky reflecting the chill of the wind, watching the clouds cry, how could I be, a reflection of life, wheathering wethering whethering away, here today gone tomorrow, to live another day, born under the stars, and moon, a reflection of life watching the earth bloom, so beautiful life has become, a reflection of life, living under the sun, the moon, the earth, and sun working as one, what would life become without one another, what would life be without the birth of father and mother, loving birth, life, father and thy mother, giving hope, love, and thankfulness to thy loving brother, a reflection of life, and love from thy loving mother, watching lives reflection in the light of day as day becomes night, and night becomes day, life is all one in the same, a reflection of life in mourning dew, once again born again, tears of rain, reflection of life, watching life be born again.

KG

1-7-15

Heaven is where ever I am for I am the one to bring forth happiness.

KG

Life, creation from ones creator who attracted your mold of life, like star dust which in turn brought a new son to life, like life which in turn brings fourth eternal light, what is yet unseen is in turn brought fourth to light, unity in form is in turn a form of life, darkness is the true opposite of ones form of light, what once was dark shall now be brought to light, a perfect creation of life to light in sight, if one can unveil the true meaning to ones true meaning of the perfect creation of life, one will then in turn, turn what is known to be true to light, and bring what is unknown to life, like the sun above who in turn brings fourth the light, revealing in turn the true meaning to life, let what once was dark in turn, turn to light, and bring fourth what is to be unknown to life, understanding the meaning to my life and the mold to life, what once was dark is now seen by light.

KG

So much talent in the world, sometimes it's hard to see, a shining star like me. Thankful for those who see the better side of me.

KG

No more tears for those who lost love, there has to be more to life, then this constant push and shove, pouring out liquor for the stars above, here is heaven in a bottle from me with love, I can never forget those I hold close, I love much more then most. These tears are for you, heart deeper then the ocean blue, baby this world's for you. What once was can be a loving memory for you from me.

KG

Feeling so alone, and separate from life, surrounded by a sea of people, tell me. Lord why do the winds deceive me.

KG

I don't understand, how something so beautiful such as a woman can take the life of a <u>MAN</u>

KG

I hope for happiness, so why do they wish me??? a man between life and death, I won???

Poem: 12-8-12

Beautiful

And you can have this life of mine, tared, and torn by life. And you can have this heart of mine, cold and lifeless, compared to you, I value none, a life full of heart attack and heartbreak, shadowed by death, and weighed down by the stress of the world, longing for someone as beautiful as you, may I fall in love with you, I would leave it all for you, would I be insulting if I said I love you, a star to shine bright, like a moth to a flame I'm attracted to light, like the moon and sun that brings light to life, a beauty beyond sight, a miracle of life beyond my reflection in the mirror, my clarity in the mist of sadness, could this be the end of the madness, the beginning of the end of ones heart so cold, wiping away tears older then time, I would gladly trade my life, for this beauty of mine, my own star to shine, with her on arm this world feels limitless, a warming of a heart so heartless take hold this life of mine, turn by time, restless in space until this beauty's mine. Hold on tight, and I'll never let go, she's priceless in every way, as real as flesh can be, I imagine an image of her along side of me. I wonder if I can bring this fantasy to life, she feels as real as me, longing for what could be, but how does one catch a shooting star flying faster then light, powerful enough to turn day to night, a gift of <u>life</u>, to bring my heart to <u>life</u>. <u>I offer you my heart, and the key to me, and my worthless life</u>. Separate from the pain that stains the soul, she's perfection, as perfect as time, I am now willing <u>to give up this life of mine</u>.

KG

Poem: 12-12-12

Alone

Alone again, gone, and forgotten, the end seems close to me, empty, and hollow draped in the skin I'm in, a shell of what once was, a fration of self, my life seems to be just a memory, how could the light of life remember me, just a memory to be, just a memory of me, left with nothing, where did the substance of life go, carried away by the winds, as the winds blow, to and fro, where did my life go. So empty, and hollow, waiting for the winds to blow life my way, so empty inside today, hoping the stress, and strife of life fly way, and to begin again, with the smell of promise in the wind, will this emptiness of life lead me astray, to end again as my ashes of life fly away, tempted by death with black clouds over head, remembering exactly with heart to what the winds said, Happiness is in the heart of the ones who keep love close to heart if this is the end, where do I start, loving, love as art. Alone again searching for a feeling of heart

Gone and Forgotten

From me

To you

Here's a piece of my heart

KG

Poem: 12-15-12

Pleasure and pain, as the rain comes my way, hoping we live to die another day, will when the madness end, trapped by memories of the past, praying for hope, and good fortune, searching for the key to happiness to erase the madness that lies within, buried between the skin I'm in, waiting for good time to surface once again, tempted by sin, as my words of wisdom are blown away by the wind, hoping never to sin again. I'm only flesh, and bone as my torment, and madness roams free. Listening deeply to what these wise words showed me. There is no winning between the lines of life and death, life controlled by faith time, and space lined by the worlds' attraction to life, enduring lives pleasures and pain until the end of life, as the rains come. Show me the way to heaven's gate, and watch me disappear into paradise after life, tell me <u>why must one suffer to enjoy the true pleasures of life</u>. Waiting for happiness to come my way. Knowing this pain and torment will end before lives end watching the rainfall again, praying for happiness before the end as my life is washed away by the wind until I begin again.

12-20-12

Beyond the looking glass, an image that brightens the soul, a love yet to hold, a connection as old as time, will you be mine, beyond the looking glass lies a love older then time, older them rhythm and rhyme, her beauty never changes unlike the sands of time, could she be mine, this beauty that lies beyond the looking glass, thinking of loves face as the years past, knowing love to last eternally, generations past, while my beauty remains the same, love more beautiful than the sweetest wine, more nourishing the lifes rain, with beauty strong enough to numb the strongest pain, this beauty of mine, valued more then this life of mine, my reflection of life beyond the looking glass, loving how her beauty remains as our years pass.

KG

12-23-12

You told me your heart was meant for me, I thought we were meant to be, I thought my heart was meant for you, soul mates to be, you said I was the light of your life, meant for life to share, promising a heart meant not to share, like the moon colliding with the sun to become one, what would life be like without the moon, and sun. You told me I could love you for life, instead you but a price tag on a much priceless life. I thought you were mine until the end of time, when I wished to share with you this life of mine. Do you wish me gone and forgotten before the sunshine. I thought your heart was as warm as mine. Mrs. Bitter Sweet, life without love like yours will leave me brittle and weak. Loves gone but never forgotten, I thought I was meant for you, and you were meant for me, because we were meant to be, but you told me your heart was never meant for me, so cold and heartless, how could this be. I guess I was meant for you, but you were never meant for me.

KG

A day late and a dollar short, watching my dreams fly right out the window. Money on my mind like rain, sleat, hail, and snow, looking down at my life wondering where did the time go, where did my mind go, running in circles day after day, watching my life float away, where were you when the rains came, just look at what I became, battered, scared, and slaved, ain't no more love for me, holding close to promises of the past, but we all you know that promises don't last, stuck in the future, caught by the past watching the hours past, tell me how long will this pain last, I bring up love, but they bring up the past, falling in love with the pain, drowning in the rain of my own sorrows. Stuck in the wind, knowing I can win, again, and again, but will when the pain end, how could you forget me, when will you forgive me. This man of flesh, without you there's nothing left, and I'm running out of breath, will you remember me, when I'm gone. Here until thy father calls me home GOODBYE love I'm GONE, (but never forgotten) a day late and a dollar short.

12-28-13

Surrounded by a sea of strangers, now older in years. Alone and forgotten by men that fellow press. Starting to feel the winter I haven't seen in years. How cold is the world that turns, shining in the brightness of life that brightly burns. Darkness to light, and light to dark, will it ever be my turn, a companion of life and love, a better half, I give all of me to you never half, surrounded by life and you're all I have.

KG

Laughing at my ignorance so close to Gods hands. Engulfed by time, where does the time go? Twice the man I used to be, feeling time pre through me cursing my mortal soul, searching for immortality, praying the answer lies at the bottom of my own ale, how do you hult death and deaths foul smell, laughing at the end of this bottle of this fine old ale, eight bottles after me, how many more must I manage, sitting with 9 answers with more knowledge to absorb, right is right now seeing the reasons why I soak my brain, laughing uncontrollable at my cure to mortality, knowing the smell of death doesn't taste night, feeling one with God, staring at the reflection of my own answers, God, forgive me for I have sinned, and I probably will again, and over again. Laughing at life, time bending me over again, tell me how can I win, if I was born in sin.

Paralyzed, frozen in fear, smoothened by the light of night, as the witching hour draws nears. I hear the sound death haunting me. Echoing in the distance, closer a closer comes the sounds of death, attracted to beat of my own heart, like a moth to the brightest. The souls beneath me rooted and bound, mesmerize by life and death. Holding ever so closely and breath, is this revenge or is this justice that controls my life and death, still remaining still??? unmoved <u>without</u> rope or chain. Soaked by the tears of night, closer and closer and ever so near, the sound of metal against metal that draws ever so near, wishing for life, a life without fear, promises of a <u>beating</u> heart echoing on the light of night, a fugitive of life awaiting the reaper as <u>sadness</u> continues to fall, like winter rain, sharp and cold, piercing the fabric of my very own soul, the lights of a locomotive taunting me and my existence, closer and closer unbroken and unchanged comes the sounds of death, still and unchanged in my sound of breath. Why can't I break free from this madness, it is life that haunts me, nothing more and, nothing less said the sounds of death; closer and closer it comes as I brace for the light of night gone but not forgotten saved by heavens light.

Should I follow the sun or the moon?

Older with every step I take, watching life take its toll on me, problems around every corner and every bend. What a beautiful life, a seed only becomes prosperist if it's nourcured right, watching beautiful blossoms following and knowing the way of the light, does everything beautiful follow the shine of the light. So many thoughts and dreams left unseen by <u>eye</u>, consumed by knowledge explaining why we live and <u>die</u>, soul searching the <u>sky</u>, for a beautiful diamond in the <u>sky</u>, should <u>I</u> follow the sun or the moon watching life unfold like a flower in bloom, we reap and then we sow, like promises of life to watch, water, and grow. Why doesn't life discriminate against the coldest of heart, sitting on my throne watching life destroy the purist of heart, watching death, turn death into beauty and art. Sitting on the mountain top watching beauty destroy the coldest of hearts, watching the rotating <u>cycle</u> <u>of</u> <u>revenge</u> turn round and round, <u>eat</u> or be <u>eating</u>, such promises shall never appeal to the purist of hearts, should I follow the sun or the moon, sitting on the mountain top watching life turn death, and then in turn life consumes. Shedding tears like the change of moon, which way to turn still stuck between the sun and the moon.

Poem 10-24-14

A billion miles from nowhere, with no place to lay my head, memories of those loved that have fallen, running through the mazes in my head. I must be going mad, remembering all of the memories inplanted in my head, remembering all of the promises said, I was promised the moon and the stars, instead I'm left with the bitter aftertaste of happiness, I promise to be what I promise to be, giving more love from the pit of the loniness from the bottom of my heart, haunted by the faces of the past, a billion miles from nowhere with no release from the sadness. I'm only human, I don't know if I can conquer the theroniness and the endlessness of madness, a billion miles, a billion miles, where did the time go. I must be losing touch with reality, where did my mind go, lost in space without a paddle walking on cosmic dust what do you <u>love most</u> in life love or lust dust. The battle between Heaven and Hell is the only word I trust, trying to fill the emptiness inside, still in love with yesterday, feeling my emptiness of heart from a billion miles away, I was told time heals all wounds, but I am still torn, is sadness the cure for my madness, or should I just let go lost and unwanted a billion miles from nowhere. I wonder if I should just let go, lost but not forgotten.

Sometimes it's so hard to find the words to say. Standing face to face with a mirror image of perfection, a beauty beyond beauty, so pure, untainted, untouched, and untamed. A spirit free untouched, and unstained by the pain of life, a beauty only matched by heavens light, standing face to face with impurity, stained by grief. Can beauty free a wounded soul, filled with the cold heartedness of life, shadowed by the ghost of the past. Please save me. Has freedom come at last. Could this be the other half to my seamlessly meaningless life, like the sun that brings forth life to what's living. Save me, and end this unjustist that I call life my opposite. Face to face with perfection without the right words to say. I don't know why saying I love you now seems so hard to say. Standing face to face with perfection without words to say I Love You.

A million miles away from you, away from you floating amongst the stars. A millions miles away from you, away from you wondering where you are, I remember you standing near to me. I hope this isn't just a memory, I remember who you are, a priceless smile shining bright amongst the stars. I wonder if you remember me because I remember who you are, I can't stand you not near to me, I long to have you here with me, wondering where you are. A million miles away from you. A million miles away.

Poem 02-2-15

I've never lost, as much as I lost today. Some would say, this is the price that bosses pay. But I would say, today is just another day, but I've never lost, as much as I lost today but tomorrow is another day.

???

Is it all an illusion, blinded by lifes delusion of life and love, how could something so false feel so real. What a fool I must be, hoping the truth of life and love would set me free, what a fool I must be, consuming lies and deceit wondering why this world sickens me, plagued by lies and mystery, with the eyes of agelessness. Nothing can pains the soul like the truth, still blinded by illusion, ignorance is such bliss. Mocked by the figure that lies in secret tell me, how priceless is the truth, and how does one put a price on love, materialistic untruths hold no value, meaningless objects that lure me astray, delusions of life and love, cursed I am, cursed with this beating heart of mine, blinded by beauty's life and limb, what a fool I must be, thinking love, could ever love me, is it love that sickens me, let the truth be told, feeling as old as the oak tree, still blinded by love, waiting for life to set me free. I can't believe life would make a fool of me. But then I <u>remember love is a part of life, and life is just a mystery</u>. Or is it all an illusion.] I find myself feeling so empty, I trying to hold on to this emptiness, this nothingness that surrounds me, alone and hollow, holding on to the past, ignorance is bliss, but how long does innocents last, blinded by life, and love, watching lifes delusions past, yes dear, I'll be here when the hours pass, is love just an illusion I dare to ask.

11-5-14

I am nothing, holding on to nothingness, that why I sometimes <u>Slip and Fall</u>

KG

It is the unjust that judge me, more often than not. Blinded by the truth of life, what reflection of life distorts the truth that I see, how could life be blinded by the unjust and unfair. Life without rule, the way of the savage, and brimstone coats the air. What should happen if I tell a lie, cut from the same cloth, there is no difference in the color of bloodshed, there is no difference in death, belittled by status, and stature, rank, and religion, the blind leading the blind, preaching words of righteousness and wisdom, reducing truth to lies, where does the balance lie, dare I <u>ask</u>, the present is only the present because of the lies from the <u>past</u> how did the unjust become just or dare I ask.

Is it God the one, to come and take his love away, or was it the devil that has come to play. Feeling the weight of the world on my shoulders. Winter is near, feeling the breath of a new season, temptation around every corner. What lies around the corner ahead. Floating through life as a transparent image from the past. Where does one go from here. Blinded by destiny, and fate. It is God, or the Devil that has come to take me. Bond by honor, and courage, and the will to except the fate that blankets me. My true test of fate. Standing in front of those righteous enough to judge. I have only to fear God, and nothing else, hoping the devil hasn't come to play.

I can feel the end closing with no light in sight hoping life in the after life stuck in the dark waiting for gleamer of light. There's no room out there for me, no space to breath no room to grow, no way out no truth to the life I live only lies and deception falsehood and fiction, no truth in the life I live except for the life I live ??? trapped by lies that cross the lines of life, hoping for life in the afterlife with no end in ??? light hoping for the end to close in and take away the lies that surrounds me a life of lies that creep up to drown me ??? while I can feel the end closing in with no end in sight hoping for end of torment and strains of life hoping for a life with??? reason a life with more meaning??? than this hoping for much more??? more life than this. Surrounded by lies with no end hoping for something better waiting at my end I can feel the end closing in waiting for something better than the life I'm in.

Poem 10-27-2019

I can still remember watching the sand falling through the hour glass.

I can still remember my life slipping right out of my hands.

Staring through the open window of wisdom fate and destiny.

I can still remember closing my eyes just to watch the pain fade away.

The only way to defeat pain is torcher until life comes to bring relief to end the pain.

The end of pain and the voices in my head seems so far away.

Still surrounded by madness searching for the answers to my mystery.

KG

Poem 11-24-2019

Why do I still feel like I'm still trapped in that crystal ball

Staring at my reflection searching for a way out.

Stuck in a world full of mystery magic and memories of what once was.

I was pushed out the box by fantasy magic and make believe

I exist, I am more than make believe.

Created by existence and time born staring at the stars with my head in the clouds.

This can't be make believe

This feels like magic

As real as time

Surrounded by memories still trapped by the reflection created by my imagination pushed out the box by fantasy magic and memories of what once was. So why do I feel like I'm still trapped in that crystal ball.

(December's Ninth) and all's well 12-09-2019

Once upon a drafty summers night.

Staring into the shadows, through the mist

I saw a ghostly figure floating under the midsummers moon light and once again

I looked again hoping to once again catch hint to that ghostly figure haunting me amongst the shadows that very night. And once again there was no one there again today about 8 days from Independence Day 2 months after May. So once again I looked again, and yet again there was no one there again today.

Once upon a December's 9th

KG

I watch the tide fell back as the moon turns and fades away.

And when the world crumbled and fades away.

I will be here standing.

KG

Alternative song

Poem 01-10-2020

I am more than mortal

I can feel the rage and hate from below and above.

Followed by black clouds in the sky waiting to bring the rain upon me.

Soaked by these tears that bring life to life. Still fighting the rage against the machine.

I wonder the earth in search for belief

Surrounded by invisible cockroaches and transparent rats on a string.

I am immortal

I am immortal

I am immortal

I am immortal

I spread my wings and take flight

Somewhere in the atmosphere somewhere

Poem 1-5-2020

I have the world up my sleeves.

I am the man until infinity and beyond.

I can part the oceans and the seas.

I am the man, and I stand tall

I am stronger than life permits

I'll be here standing even after the world starts to fall apart and even after the sunsets and the winds come and take me away.

I will be standing.

I will become immortal

I will be free

I will become more than a memory.

Watching the sands of time fade away

I will be the one to let the world lean on me.

I will become greater than the stories told of me.

I watch the stars in the distant shine and twinkle as the skies light proving I'm guided by life somewhere in a distant galaxy.

Amongst the <u>stars</u>, the moon the sun and Jupiter and Mars.

I am immortal

Peace attracts hate and saving myself seems insane when insanity surrounds me.

I am immortal

Somebody please come and take this pain away.

Why should I ever give a helping hand when their hatred for me still remains?

I am immortal trapped by these pearly gates please allow me to come forth to cleanse the world and take this pain away

I am immortal

I am immortal

I am immortal

I am more than mortal!!!

KG

Poem song 01-10-2020

I tried to give you the world and you took all of me.

I'll lend you my heart just to have you break it every time.

I wrote a new song just for you and quote ever line.

I taken by your beauty

I tried to give you the world and you took all of me.

I wanted to hold your hand for ever

Just to watch you let go and walk away.

Why do women tell lies?

I tried to give you the world and you took all of me.

I'll lend you my heart just to have you break it every time

I wrote this song just for you and continue to quote even line and I still love you so

I saw you enter the crowd and let go, and I still love you so. That's why I sorry you had to go.

Printed in the United States
By Bookmasters